It was a sunny day. Jelly was playing in the lane. She saw a ring with a blue jewel glinting in the sun.

Jelly picked it up. Oh no! The blue jewel fell out of the ring and rolled away on the path.

A magpie flew down and picked it up. The magpie flew away with the blue jewel in its beak.

The magpie took the blue jewel back to its nest in a tall tree. Then the wind blew.

The wind blew the magpie and its nest out of the tall tree. The blue jewel fell on to the long grass.

The next day a rabbit came to chew the long blades of grass. She saw the blue jewel glinting with dew.

She picked it up and took it back to her burrow. Then she fell asleep with the blue jewel next to her.

A little shrew saw the blue jewel and picked it up. He ran out of the rabbit's burrow and away down the lane.

Jelly was in the lane. She saw the shrew and ran after him. The little shrew dropped the blue jewel.

Jelly picked it up. "Here is a new blue jewel, just like the old one," she said. "It is my lucky day."

"ew"

jewel

blew

flew

chew

shrew

new

dew

High Frequency Words

it was a day playing in the
she up no of and away on
said like to he is my

saw with out down took back
tree then next her little ran
after him just one here came
old